How Does It Feel?

Seed Learning

smooth

rough

hard

squishy

warm

cool

wet

dry

How does it feel?

It feels hard.

How does it feel?

It feels squishy.

How does it feel?

It feels rough.

How does it feel?

It feels wet.

How does it feel?

It feels cool.

How does it feel?

It feels smooth.

Let's learn more about Mexico.

Tamale